OCTOPUSES

A Buddy Book by
Deborah Coldiron

ABDO
Publishing Company

UNDERWATER WORLD

VISIT US AT
www.abdopublishing.com

Published by ABDO Publishing Company, 8000 West 78th Street, Edina, Minnesota 55439.

Coordinating Series Editor: Sarah Tieck
Contributing Editor: Michael P. Goecke
Graphic Design: Deborah Coldiron
Cover Photograph: Brandon Cole Marine Photography
Interior Photographs/Illustrations: Clipart.com (page 9); Brandon Cole Marine Photography (pages 17, 19, 27, 28, 29); Corbis (page 5); Deep-Sea Photography (page 12); Getty Images/AFP: Handout/Handout (page 17); ImageMix (pages 17, 21, 23); Minden Pictures: Fred Bavendam (pages 7, 15); Photos.com (pages 11, 16, 17, 21, 30); Jeff Rotman Photography (page 25); Professor Albert Titus, University at Buffalo (page 30)

Library of Congress Cataloging-in-Publication Data

Coldiron, Deborah, 1973-
      Octopuses/Deborah Coldiron.
          p. cm.—(Underwater World)
      Includes index.
      ISBN 978-1-59928-815-4
        1. Octopuses—Juvenile literature. I. Title.

      QL430.3.O2C65 2007
      594.56—dc22

                                                                                    2007014852

Table Of Contents

The World Of Octopuses

Every living creature needs water. Some animals not only need water, they live in it, too.

Scientists have found more than 250,000 kinds of plants and animals living underwater. And, they believe there could be one million more! The octopus is one animal that lives in this underwater world.

Seventy percent of Earth's surface is covered in water. Octopuses make this underwater world their home.

Octopuses are smart creatures. But, they are best known for their soft bodies and eight arms.

There are around 300 known kinds of octopuses on Earth. Octopuses come in many sizes. The smallest octopus is about one inch (3 cm) wide from arm tip to arm tip. The largest may grow up to 20 feet (6 m) wide!

Most octopuses are bottom dwellers. They hide in rocky or rough areas of the ocean floor.

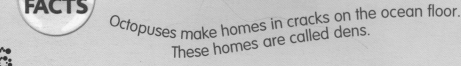

Octopuses make homes in cracks on the ocean floor. These homes are called dens.

The world's largest octopus is the giant Pacific octopus.

Meet And Greet

Octopuses are **invertebrates**. The main part of an octopus's body is globe shaped. It is called a mantle.

Octopuses have eight long arms. Each arm has two rows of suction cups called suckers. An octopus uses its suckers to grab, feel, and taste objects.

The Body Of An Octopus

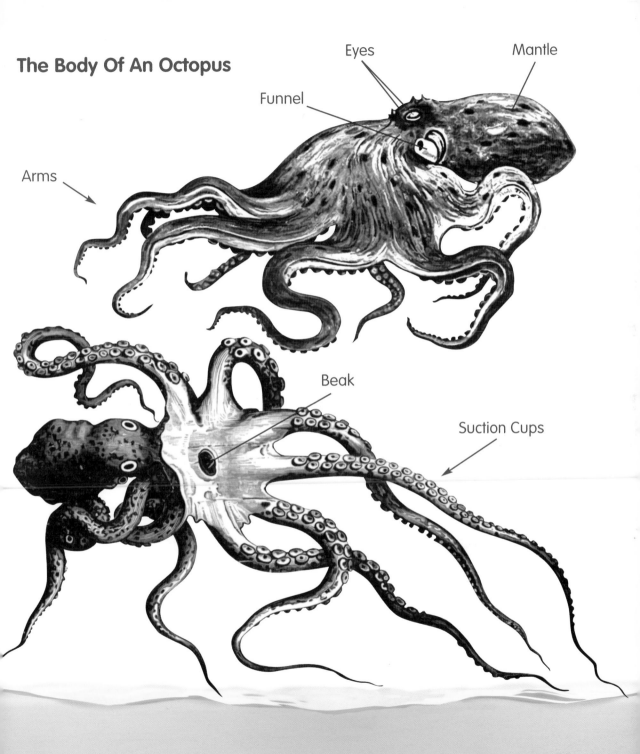

Eyes

Mantle

Funnel

Arms

Beak

Suction Cups

Most octopuses use their arms to move along the ocean floor. To move quickly, an octopus takes water into its mantle. Then, it squeezes the water out through a tube called a funnel. Scientists call this type of motion "jet propulsion."

An octopus's mouth is surrounded by its many arms. Its mouth has a hard beak. An octopus uses its beak to break open shells. It also tears off pieces of flesh from its **prey** with its beak.

FAST FACTS

Octopuses have no bones in their bodies. These soft-bodied invertebrates can squeeze through holes as small as their beaks!

An octopus's eyes are similar to a person's eyes. Scientists say octopuses have very good eyesight.

Octopuses also have well-developed brains. Scientists have seen them learn to move through mazes!

Octopuses also use their funnels to force out water when breathing.

Funnel

13

Cirrate Octopuses

A small number of octopus **species** have fins on their mantles! These unusual creatures are called cirrate octopuses. They live deep in the ocean. The most well-known cirrate octopus is the Dumbo octopus.

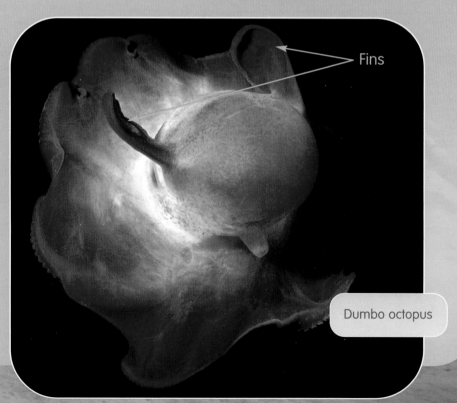

Fins

Dumbo octopus

A Growing Octopus

An octopus's eggs are round, like grapes. They are held together in strands of 100 or more.

After laying her eggs, a mother octopus hangs the strands from her den ceiling. It takes a few weeks for the mother to do this. When she is done, she has thousands of eggs to look after.

During this time, the mother octopus does not leave the den. She cleans her eggs. And often, the mother octopus gently moves water across them. This provides a constant supply of oxygen to the eggs.

The eggs of some octopus **species** hatch in a few weeks. Others take months.

When young octopuses hatch, they float to the surface. There, they join many other floating creatures known as plankton. After a few weeks, the surviving octopus babies return to the ocean floor.

Octopus mothers carefully guard their eggs.

Once on the bottom, octopuses are ready to begin their **solitary** lives. They will become hunters and masters of **disguise**.

Family Fun

Octopuses belong to a group of animals called cephalopods. Cephalopods have soft bodies and many arms. They are some of the most intelligent creatures in the sea.

There are around 800 known **species** of cephalopods. This group also includes squid, nautiluses, and cuttlefish.

Cuttlefish are known for quickly changing color. They have a hard plate inside their bodies. This is called a cuttlebone.

The flamboyant cuttlefish is small but deadly. It is only about two inches (5 cm) long, but its flesh is toxic.

Unlike other cephalopods, nautiluses have a hard shell. Some have as many as 90 arms! Their arms do not have suckers.

Squid can shoot out ink.

Look how small the fisherman's hands are compared to this squid!

The largest of all cephalopods is the colossal squid. It can grow to 46 feet (14 m) long! The squid pictured here was caught by fishermen in early 2007. It weighed close to 1,000 pounds (450 kg)!

Squid have eight arms and two longer feeding tentacles. These bullet-shaped creatures are fast swimmers.

Friends And Neighbors

Octopuses live alone. But, they have many neighbors.

Octopuses that live near coral reefs share their **habitat** with **sea anemones**, corals, and sea sponges. Clown fish, parrot fish, and sharks live there as well. Coral reefs are also home to eels, sea snakes, and sea turtles.

Mimic Octopus

One amazing octopus actually imitates its neighbors! The mimic octopus can pretend to be a **venomous** sea snake or a poisonous flatfish. Sometimes it copies a deadly scorpion fish or even a stingray. These behaviors help protect it.

These mimic octopuses are pretending to be a banded sea snake *(right)* and a poisonous flatfish *(below)*.

Ocean Hunters

Most octopuses are nighttime hunters. They feed on creatures such as scallops, clams, and snails. They also eat **crustaceans** (kruhs-TAY-shuhns) such as crabs and shrimp. Some octopuses eat fish or even other octopuses.

FAST FACTS

Octopuses often take their dinner home to eat! Divers have seen piles of empty shells stacked up outside octopus dens. These piles are called middens.

Crabs *(above)*, shrimp *(right)*, and snails *(below)* are among the foods that octopuses eat.

Octopuses are very capable predators. Many have **venom** in their **saliva**. A bite from an octopus's beak can deliver this venom to prey. The venom **paralyzes** the animal.

Some prey, such as clams, have hard shells. An octopus uses its beak or rough tongue to make a hole in the shell. It forces a fluid through the hole. This fluid begins to break down the prey's body. Then, the octopus can suck out its dinner.

Blue Ring Octopus

The blue ring octopus only grows to a few inches wide. It is not **aggressive** by nature. But, it is one of the most poisonous animals in the ocean. Its **paralyzing venom** is more powerful than any land animal's venom. In fact, this little creature has enough poison to kill a human!

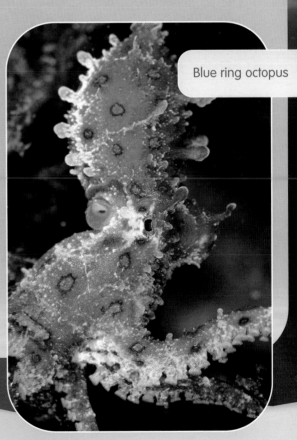

Blue ring octopus

Escape Artists

Many animals eat octopuses. These predators include moray and conger eels, dolphins, seals, whales, stingrays, and sharks.

Octopuses have special tricks to protect them from predators. Their bodies can help them hide and escape.

FAST FACTS Although octopuses are great at matching their skin to their surroundings, scientists believe they are actually color-blind!

26

Octopuses have ink sacs inside their bodies. When they are in danger, they can shoot ink into the water. It turns clear water cloudy. This helps them escape.

Sometimes, divers get too close to octopuses. To mask its escape, an octopus might shoot ink into the water.

Some octopuses shed their arms to escape! The arms continue to wiggle after falling off. This draws attention away from the octopus. Then, it can jet quickly to safety.

Octopuses also use their skin to hide from predators. An octopus can change its skin color and **texture**. These tricks help it blend into its surroundings. This ability is called camouflage.

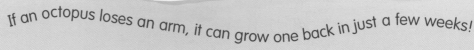

An octopus's skin is naturally somewhat smooth. But if it is hiding near coral, an octopus can look very rough and bumpy. Amazingly, these two images show the same octopus.

Fascinating Facts

The Caribbean reef octopus traps prey with its webbed arms.

⋇ The Caribbean reef octopus has webbing between its arms. It resembles an open umbrella. The octopus uses this webbing like a net to trap its prey.

⋇ Some octopuses occasionally walk on just two of their eight arms. This frees them to use the other six arms to **disguise** themselves!

🐙 Octopuses are capable of learning many things. Scientists say they can learn to recognize and choose between different shapes. Some can even open jars with lids to get treats!

🐙 Some octopuses have been known to prop up rocks outside of their dens. Just like locking your front door, this helps protect the octopus as it sleeps.

Octopuses use objects, such as rocks and sand dollar skeletons, to cover their den openings.

Learn And Explore

Professor Albert Titus studies how octopuses see. He works at the University at Buffalo in New York.

Titus used his research to create an electronic eye. His invention is called the o-retina. It is based on the octopus's eye.

One day, the o-retina may be used in underwater robots to explore the ocean!

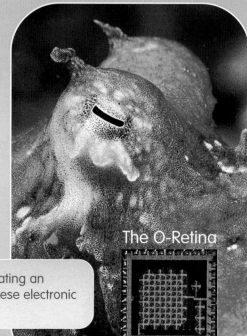

The O-Retina

Titus is planning to expand his studies by creating an electronic eagle eye. He hopes to combine these electronic eyes to create new levels of robotic sight.

IMPORTANT WORDS

aggressive   a determination to pursue something.

crustacean   any of a group of animals with hard shells that live mostly in water. Crabs, lobsters, and shrimp are all crustaceans.

disguise   to change the appearance of to prevent recognition.

habitat   a place where a living thing is found.

invertebrate   an animal without a backbone.

paralyze   to make something unable to move.

saliva   a liquid produced by the body that keeps the mouth moist.

sea anemone   an attached marine animal with stinging tentacles around its mouth opening.

solitary   alone.

species   living things that are very much alike.

texture   the way something feels.

venom   poison.

WEB SITES

To learn more about octopuses, visit ABDO Publishing Company on the World Wide Web. Web sites about octopuses are featured on our Book Links page. These links are routinely monitored and updated to provide the most current information available.

www.abdopublishing.com

INDEX